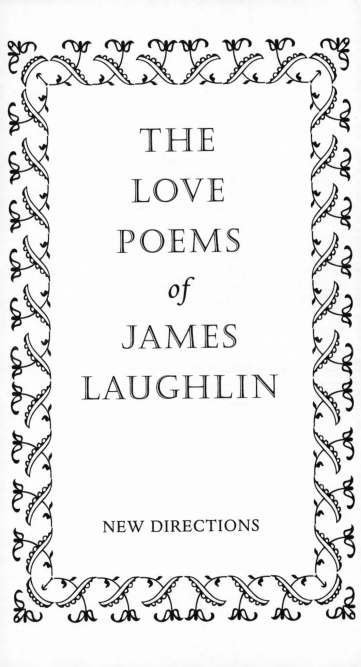

THE
LOVE
POEMS
of
JAMES
LAUGHLIN

NEW DIRECTIONS

Manufactured in the United States of America
New Directions Books are printed on acid-free paper.
First published clothbound by New Directions in 1997
and as New Directions Paperbook 865 in 1998
Published simultaneously in Canada by
Penguin Books Canada Limited

Library of Congress Cataloging-in-Publication Data

Laughlin, James.   1914–1997
    [Poems.   Selections]
    The love poems of James Laughlin.
        p.   cm.
    ISBN 0-8112-1387-0
    I. Love poetry, American. I. Title.
    PS3523.A8245A6   1997
    811´.54—dc21   97-10980
SECOND PRINTING   CIP

New Directions books are published for James Laughlin
by New Directions Publishing Corporation,
80 Eighth Avenue, New York, NY 10011

THE LOVE POEMS
OF JAMES LAUGHLIN

For Gertrude

Why Does Love Happen?

It's not so simple
As the biological imperative
To propagate the race.
There's that, of course,
But it's also the way you look
At me, your face alight with joy
And the way your voice sounds
In the dark. What makes *your* love
Choose me? Once I asked you
But you wouldn't answer.
It was your secret. Keep it so.

The Atman of Sleep

You had fallen asleep beside
me and your closed eyes in

the dusklight were so beauti-
ful   the fingers of one hand

were curled like a child's
against your cheek   I listened

for the cadence of your breathing
and made mine come & go with

yours one breath for both of us.

Atman—Sanskrit: breath, soul.

The Sinking Stone

High in the alpine
snowfields when a

stone slips from a
peak and rolls to

the glacier below
the sun will heat

it in the burning
days of spring and

it will melt itself
a hole & disappear

in the snow   I like
that stone burned

hot from loving you
am sinking deep in-

to a cold vast no-
where ice land of

your loving someone
else instead of me!

for Maria

The Daze of Love

Comes often from
the blaze of light
when an asteroid
passes us too near.

There is also
the softer radiance
when we are separated
and sink into sleep
thinking of each other.

You Were Asleep

when I came to bed all
curled up like a child

under the blanket and
when I slipped in be-

side you as quietly as
I could you stirred but

didn't really wake and
stretched out a hand to

cup my face as if you were
holding a bowl or a ball.

for Ann

I Want to Breathe

you in   I'm not talking about
perfume or even the sweet

odor of your skin but of the
air itself   I want to share

your air inhaling what you
exhale   I'd like to be that

close   two of us breathing
each other as one as that.

The Nameless Voyage

Where does she go
when she closes her eyes
when we are making love?

She is there by my side
yet she isn't there

If I touch her she trembles
but says nothing

One night I asked her
where it was she travelled

This time she smiled and
answered don't be worried

I'll never be far from you
The land which I visit

is the land of the poems
you have written for me.

The Enlacement

There's something holy about
falling asleep pressed close

against a beloved   is it a sur-
vival from some primitive rite

it's more than the huddling
together of animals in the

storm   is one body a sanctu-
ary for another   the enlace-

ment's a vow for the future
a pledge not to be broken

now blood touches blood and
breath breath as if they were

hands touching and holding.

In Half Darkness

your face is still so beautiful
there is a different radiance

that comes in sleep   I wake and
touch your cheek   I feel your

breath on my groping fingers
your eyes are closed but I sus-

pect they can see & are watch-
ing what is to come   they are

looking into the future as far
as the end of our time together.

Rhyme

Isn't it good she asked (as
if there were no question in

the question) that we love
each other's bodies   one big

one small   one slim   one tall
isn't it good that we love the

way our skins taste the way
they feel to touch & stroke

of course I love you for your
mind and you me for my dispo-

sition but aren't we very lucky
our bodies love each other too?

The Unanswerable Question

It's easy to oblige you
when you say your whole

body wishes to be touching
all of mine from forehead

to feet   but what of the
soul   how can we realize

the soul   what is its lo-
cus   where does it reside?

The Importance of Silence

Because there are some things
for which there are no names

there is no need for you to
try to invent them   your words

from the old poets are beauti-
ful to read on the page but the

ones I want to hear & feel come
from your lips and your hands.

A Translation

How did you decide to translate me
from one language to another   let's

say from the English of friendship
to the French of lovers   we'd known

each other half a year when one day
as we were talking (it was about one

of your drawings) suddenly you curl-
ed yourself against me and drew my

lips down to yours   it was so deft
an alternance from one language to

the other as if to say yes you can
speak French to me now if you wish.

Arachne

You are the love spider
a delicate little creature

of luminous beauty   I know
you didn't spin your web

to catch me and then eat me
(I'm not an appetizing fly)

one morning I saw the dew-
drops glistening on your

web & was attracted & now
I'm simply so happy to be

in such a web   don't eat me
please but keep me alive &

let me try to amuse you
while you're not weaving.

The Dance of the Skin

Over her flesh the skin
dances   don't try to talk

about the dance of the
skin   don't say anything

at all   just lie still and
feel it move   just lie still.

I'd Like to be Putty

in your hands you must
shape me into the per-

son you can really love
I have no mirror to see

myself (it's only you I
see) so with your gentle

fingers you must mould me
as you'd like to have me be.

It Was the First Time

we had made love and I asked
her what she would like me to

do what would give her pleas-
ure   but she wouldn't tell me

she said I must find out for
myself   it would be better so.

Love's Altar

Let me bow down before
the altar of love   let

me genuflect at that sa-
cred place   it's useless

for you to protest that
this shrine is ordinary

and common to all your
sex   for me it's the lo-

cus of the sacrament   the
altar where the ritual of

the Mysteries is enacted.

Attracted by the Light

This warm evening, a very small bug
Has flown through the open window,
Landed on my head and is exploring
My hair. It tickles, but like a Jain
I'll not try to kill it. One of God's
Creatures. And am I not lucky
That at 79 I still have enough hair
To seem attractive to the bug?
You to whom I'm sending these lines,
Do you still think of me, far away
There in London as you are?
For me you are still the light.

for Vanessa

Touching

I want to touch you
in beautiful places

places that no one
else has ever found

places we found to-
gether when we were

in Otherwhere such
beautiful places.

A Suggestion

It would be nice if you
could stop talking while

you are kissing   I love
poets and their water-

falling words but one
thing at a time please.

Why Do You Never Enter My Dreams

Nightly I await you
but you do not come

the lamp burns & the
table is spread   the

Falernian is decanted
yet it is dawn and you

have not appeared   are
you afraid of my dreams

they are loving and will
not harm you   or do you

in sleep go visiting
the dreams of another?

Two Spoons

After we have made love
and are sleepy we curl

together like two spoons
each fitting closely in-

to the other   my arm is
around you my hand hold-

ing your breast   I can
even feel your feet with

my toes   your long hair
is between your back and

my chest   I whisper very
softly into your ear   for

a moment you squeeze my
fingers and we fall asleep.

The Deep Pool

I want you to plunge into my life
as if you were diving into a deep

pool in the sea   let nothing be
hidden from you   hold your breath

and swim underwater to explore
every crevice in the rock and

the coral   make your way through
the undersea vegetation question-

ing the strange creatures which
you may encounter   let the fish

gossip with you about me   ques-
tion the giant squid and the

poisonous sting ray   they can
tell you much about me (some of

which you may not like to hear)
let nothing be hidden   you must

know me as I was before you came.

Remembrance

It was too good to be changed
what we had there in Austria

that summer when we were young
(I liked it best when you wore

your dirndl and put your hair
in a long braid)   now two quite

different people will be meeting
again for the first time in many

years   different people meeting
shyly and tentatively   studying

each other with curiosity   do
you remember we'll each say   do

you remember when we swam in
the lake near Sankt Wolfgang

do you remember our walks in
the Belvedere Gardens   memo-

ries are secure   let there be
no interference from the pre-

sent and so no disappointment.

Believe Me

There can be shadows in the dark
Not many can see them
But a lover can see them
As he waits for the beloved to join him
And a lover can hear even the fall
    of a naked foot
As the beloved approaches
He can hear the soft breathing
That is rising in expectation
As he stretches out his hand in the darkness
To welcome her to the place of love.

In My Imagination

(though I am sixty now) I love
to touch you much as I did the

little girl who lived in the
house nextdoor when I was ten

touching her was a matter of
fervent curiosity to find out

how she was different and to
speculate on what the differ-

ence meant   but touching you
now (in my imagination) is

something else   it is an in-
visible act of pure affection

and my plea for reassurance
I want to be comforted by the

belief that you would want me
to love you if we were together.

Acid Rain

is falling on me again
today   it withers the

leaves on the bough and
even poisons the water in

the birdbath   it's the
acid of remembering how

badly I treated you how
cruel I was after you

were so loving to me.

The Bible Says

that Jacob had to wait
fourteen years for his

beloved Rachel   so there
is precedent in scrip-

ture for your procras-
tination   but I wish you

would make up your mind
before I'm so old that I

can't give you any fun.

Long and Languorous

A whole stolen afternoon before us
no hurry no haste   savoring every

sensation   begin perhaps with mimi-
cry of memories of adolescence

what you learned from the boy next
door what the lady who was divorced

taught me   no hurry no haste   how
is it that lovemaking from long ago

can return so vividly   we can still
feel certain touches hear certain

tones of voice even remember some
of the words exchanged   making love

is cumulative   nothing of it that
was good is really lost   and yet

there can always be discoveries
little hidden paths to pleasure

no haste no hurry   time for a mo-
ment's doze between enlacements

time even for a bit of joking be-
cause there is that aspect of the

ridiculous in coupling   better it
all be soft and slow gentle and

generous as our afternoon speeds
on its way long and languorous.

The Lost Song

This song that I have made to tell you,
"Made out of a mouthful of air,"
Who but I will ever sing it,
Who will know who made it,
Or for whom it was made?

The quoted second line is from
William Butler Yeats.

Anima Mea

After we had made love
a girl with big eyes and
warm breath started to
talk about my soul   hush
I said hush and beware
if I have soul it's
only a box of vanities
tied with frightened
pieces of string.

Love Bearing Gifts

The poet hurls so many letters at
Lucina, he is like a catapult. But
her images are so incomparable
he hopes it means that there
will be a conjunction of hearts!

The Evening Star

You came as a thought when I was
past such thinking. You came as a
song when I was finished singing.
You came when the sun had just begun
its setting. You were my evening star.

The Lighthouse

You are my lighthouse. Ceaselessly
your rotations beam over the sea
and land. Birds are guided by them
and so are travelers lost in the
moors. You are my compass and light.

Little Scraps of Love

Your letters, infrequent
But so sweet, so wandering
In what they relate, are
Little scraps of love.
What would I do without them?
They're food when I'm feeling
Hungry for you, so far away.
Please pick up your pencil
As often as you can, even if
It's only for a postcard.
And don't forget the childish
Pictures of us holding hands.

A Room in Darkness

Night is a room darkened for lovers.
The sun is gone, and our daytime
    concerns
and distractions with it.
Now in the darkness we are close
    together
As lovers are meant to be.
When we sleep or wake
Nothing intrudes between us.
We are soothed and protected
By the darkness of our room.

The first line comes from
William Carlos Williams' "Complaint."

A Secret Language

I wish I could talk to your body
Less cautiously; I mean in a
Language as forthright as its
Beauty deserves. Of course,
When we make love there is the
Communication of touch, fingers
On Flesh, lips on innermost
Flesh, but surely there must be
A kind of speech, body in body,
That is even deeper than such
Surface touching, a language
I haven't yet learned or haven't
learned well enough, hard as
I've tried. Will I ever master
That secret language for you?

Sweet Childhood

Why can't we pretend that
We're children who are
Playing with each other,
Not really understanding
What we're doing, but it's fun
It feels good and there is
An urgent curiosity to study
Each other's parts. Sweet childhood,
Happy time of innocence, come back
For us, bring back an hour
When everything was gentle and new.

There's Never a Never

in love   what once was
lovely can always return

when the storm clears or
the wind drives the clouds

away   don't be hasty don't
lock the door of your heart

there's never a never in love.

The Last Poem to Be Written

"When, when & whenever
death closes our eyes"

still shall I behold her
smiling such brightness

lady of brightness &
the illumined heart

soft walker in my blood
snow color sea sound

track of the ermine
delicate in the snow

line of the sea wave
delicate on the sand

lady of all brightness
donna del mio cuor.

*The first two lines are from
Pound's translation of
Propertius.*

CLASSIC LOVE POEMS

The Bird of Endless Time

Your fingers touch me like a bird's wing,
like the feathers of the bird that returns
every hundred years to brush against a peak
in the Himalayas until the rock's been
worn away and the kalpas are ended.

kalpas: in Hinduism an aeon.

A Classic Question

"Ingenium nobis ipsa puella facit."
Propertius wrote that it's the girl
who makes the poems. But is the obverse
true? Will poems make a girl? I'm
really not so certain about that.

—*from Sextus Propertius.*

The Coming of Spring

The Spring season is approaching,
who will help me meeting with my dearest?
How shall I describe the beauty of the dearest,
Who is immersed in all beauties,
That color all the pictures of the universe. . .

—Kabir (1440-1818),
*abridged, translation by Ezra Pound from the
English of Kali Mohan Ghose.*

The Crane

Go away, crane! Leave the garden!
You have not told my love,
the prince of the seashore,
the torment that I suffer.
Go away, crane! Leave the garden!

—*from the Tamil of Shilappadikaram,
Third Century A.D., translation by
Alain Danielou.*

The Growth of Love

I see Love grow resplendent in her eyes
with such great power and such
    noble thought
as hold therein all gracious ecstasies,
from them there moves a soul so
    subtly wrought
that all compared thereto are set
     at naught.

*—from Guido Calvacanti (1255-1300),
translation by Ezra Pound.*

The Happy Poets

It's my delight to recite
my poems in the arms of
an intelligent girl and
to please her dear ear
with what I've written.

—from Sextus Propertius.

Me iuvet in gremio doctae legisse puellae
auribus et puris scripta probasse mea

Propertius II, XIII

Her Loveliness

There where this lady's loveliness appeareth,
is heard a voice which goes before her ways
and seems to sing her name with such
    sweet praise
that my mouth fears to speak that name
    she beareth,
and my heart trembles for the grace
    she weareth.

*—from Guido Calvacanti (1255-1300),
translation by Ezra Pound.*

The Honeybee

You do everything, Melissa, just the
way your namesake the honeybee does.
When you're kissing me honey drips
from your lips, but when you ask
for money you have a sharp sting.

—*from Marcus Argentarius.*

The Locust

Locust, beguiler of my loves and
    persuader of sleep,
mimic of nature's lyre, play for me
    a tune with your
talking wings to deliver me from
    the pains of care
and of love. In the morning I'll give
    you a fresh
green leek and drops of dew sprayed
    from my mouth

—*Meleager of Gadara (flourished 60 B.C.).*

The Lovers

Radha looked on the god Krishna who
        desired only her,
who long had wanted dalliance
        with her. His face
was possessed with desire. It showed
        his passion
through tremblings of glancing eyes.
        It was like
a lotus pond with a pair of wagtails
        at play.

*—from the Hindu Gita-Govinda
(12th Century), translation by Keyt.*

The Lover's Complaint

I swear I do not ask too much:
O make that thoughtless girl
who yesterday made me
her spoils of war either love me
or let me share her bed to prove
    I love her.

—*from Ovid's* Ars Amatoria,
Horace Gregory translation.

Remembrance of Her

No man can ever pass a day in boredom
    who has remembrance of her,
for she is the beginning and birth of
    all joy: and he who
    would praise her
no matter how well he speaks of her,
    he lies!

—from the troubadour Peire Vidal
(1175-1205), translation from Provençal by
Paul Blackburn.

The Visit of Eros

Philodemus remembers how we first
    made the bedlamp
tipsy with oil, then let it go out.
    We knew there
are times when Eros wants no witness.
We had the bed, the lover's friend, to
    teach us Aphrodite's
secrets, the things of which we seldom
    dare to speak.

Printed in Giovanni Mardersteig's Dante types
Design by Jonathan Greene